Animals on the Farm

Llamas

Linda Aspen-Baxter
and Heather Kissock

MEDIA ENHANCED BOOKS
AV2 BY WEIGL™
ADDED VALUE • AUDIO VISUAL

www.av2books.com

AV² provides enriched content that supplements and complements this book. Weigl's AV² books strive to create inspired learning and engage young minds in a total learning experience.

Your AV² Media Enhanced books come alive with...

Audio
Listen to sections of the book read aloud.

Video
Watch informative video clips.

Embedded Weblinks
Gain additional information for research.

Try This!
Complete activities and hands-on experiments.

Key Words
Study vocabulary, and complete a matching word activity.

Quizzes
Test your knowledge.

Slide Show
View images and captions, and prepare a presentation.

... and much, much more!

Go to **www.av2books.com**, and enter this book's unique code.

BOOK CODE

S 8 6 8 8 5 3

AV² by Weigl brings you media enhanced books that support active learning.

Published by AV² by Weigl
350 5ᵗʰ Avenue, 59ᵗʰ Floor New York, NY 10118
Website: www.av2books.com   www.weigl.com

Library of Congress Cataloging-in-Publication Data

Kissock, Heather.
 Llamas / Heather Kissock and Linda Aspen-Baxter.
     p. cm. -- (Animals on the farm)
 ISBN 978-1-61690-930-7 (hardcover : alk. paper) -- ISBN 978-1-61690-576-7 (online)
 1. Llamas--Juvenile literature. I. Aspen-Baxter, Linda. II. Title.
 SF401.L6K57 2012
 636.2'966--dc23
                            2011023441

Printed in the United States of America in North Mankato, Minnesota
1 2 3 4 5 6 7 8 9 0 15 14 13 12 11

062011
WEP030611

Senior Editor: Heather Kissock   Art Director: Terry Paulhus

Weigl acknowledges Getty Images as the primary image supplier for this title.

Animals on the Farm
Llamas

CONTENTS

I am a large farm animal.
Farmers keep me
for my wool.
I also help protect
the farmer's sheep.

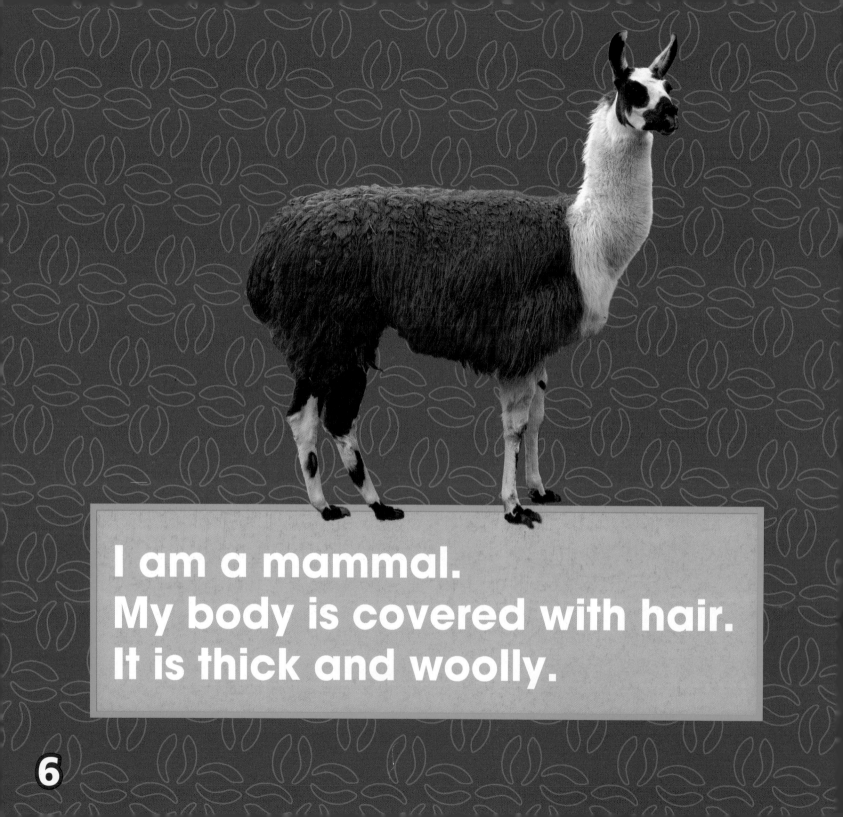

I am a mammal.
My body is covered with hair.
It is thick and woolly.

6

7

I use my four legs to walk and run. I have two toes on each foot.

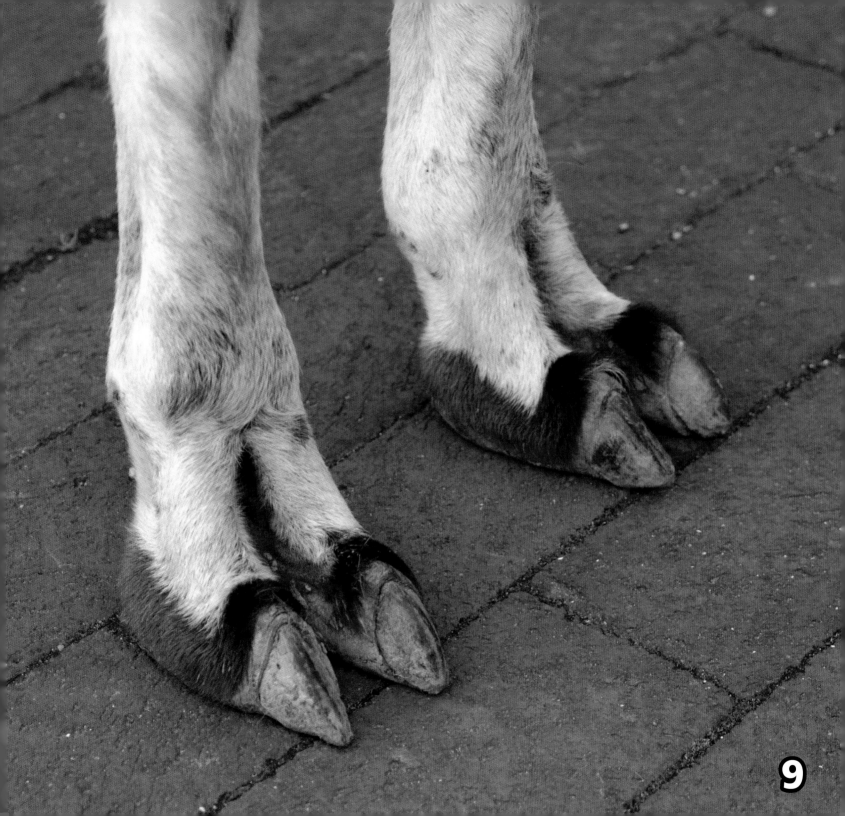

9

10

I have three eyelids and very long eyelashes. They keep dust out of my eyes.

11

I eat grass, hay, and other plants. I eat my food twice.

How do I talk to other llamas?
I hum, snort, and cluck.

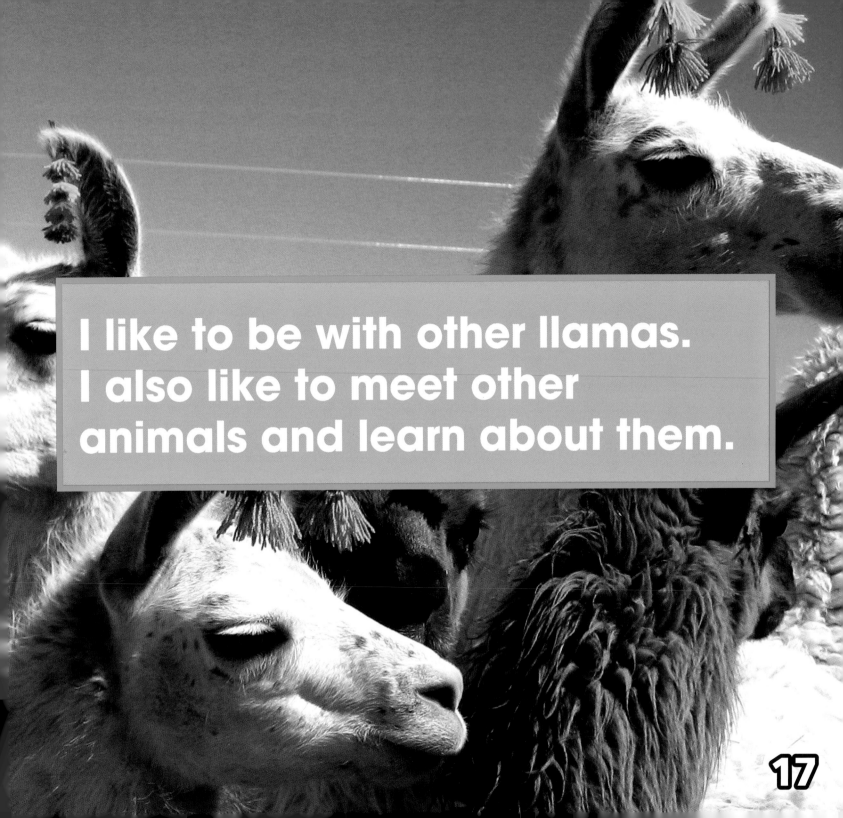

I like to be with other llamas. I also like to meet other animals and learn about them.

17

I sometimes have a baby in the spring.

18

I keep my baby close to me.

19

I smell and touch my baby with my nose. I hum to it so that it feels safe.

LLAMA FACTS

This page provides more detail about the interesting facts found in the book.
Simply look at the corresponding page number to match the fact.

Pages 4-5

Llamas are large farm animals. They are kept for their wool and to guard sheep. Llamas are also used as pack animals. Llamas can carry about 200 pounds (91 kilograms) for up to 12 hours at a time. Most llamas are sheared once every two years. Each llama produces about 7 to 8 pounds (3 to 4 kg) of fiber, or hair.

Pages 6–7

Llamas are mammals. Their bodies are covered with hair. Hair is only one feature that mammals have. All mammals are also warm-blooded. This means they are capable of producing their own body heat. As well, the female of any mammal species makes milk to feed her young.

Pages 8–9

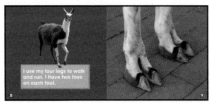

Llamas have two toes on each foot. Each toe has a toenail and pad. These features make the llama very surefooted. The pad allows the llama to grip the ground better than a hoofed animal, such as a horse. The foot pads also make llamas environmentally friendly. They leave less of an imprint on the ground than other animals.

Pages 10–11

Llamas have three eyelids and very long eyelashes. The upper and lower eyelids grow lashes. The third lash acts like a windshield wiper by wiping debris away from the llama's eye. Together, the eyelashes and eyelids help keep dust and sand out of the llama's eyes.

Pages 12–13

Llamas eat grass, hay, and other plants. They eat their food twice. Llamas are ruminants. They chew their food before swallowing it. Then, they spit it back up and chew it again. This is called chewing their cud. Llamas chew cud for eight hours a day. They have three parts to their stomach to help them break down the plants they eat.

Pages 14–15

Llamas talk to other llamas by humming, snorting, and clucking. Each sound has its own meaning. Humming is done mainly to convey concern or curiosity about something happening around them. A snort can mean the llama is in a playful mood or a warning to stay away. Llamas cluck to tell other llamas to behave themselves.

Pages 16–17

Llamas like to be with other llamas. They also like to meet other animals and learn about them. Llamas are social animals. They live in groups called herds. Llamas are very gentle by nature. They are also very curious and intelligent. Llamas will often approach a stranger and begin sniffing to get acquainted.

Pages 18–19

Llamas have their babies in the spring. A llama baby is called a cria. At birth, a cria weighs between 18 and 35 pounds (8 and 16 kg). A cria can walk one hour after birth. Llamas grow quickly. Between six months and two years of age, a cria gains about 1 pound (0.5 kg) each day.

Pages 20–21

Mother llamas smell and touch their babies with their nose. They hum to it so the baby feels safe. Young llamas stay close to their mother. They stop drinking her milk at about six months of age. Llamas are considered fully grown at three years of age.

WORD LIST

Research has shown that as much as 65 percent of all written material published in English is made up of 300 words. These 300 words cannot be taught using pictures or learned by sounding them out. They must be recognized by sight. This book contains 48 common sight words to help young readers improve their reading fluency and comprehension. This book also teaches young readers several important content words, such as proper nouns. These words are paired with pictures to aid in learning and improve understanding.

Page	Sight Words First Appearance	Page	Content Words First Appearance
4	a, also, animal, for, help, I, keep, large, me, my, the	4	farmers, sheep, wool
6	and, is, it, with	6	body, hair, mammal
8	each, four, have, on, run, to, two, use, walk	8	foot, legs, toes
11	eyes, long, of, out, they, three, very	11	dust, eyelashes, eyelids
13	eat, food, other, plants	13	grass, hay
15	do, how, talk	15	llamas
17	about, be, learn, like, them	18	baby, spring
18	in, sometimes	21	nose
19	close		
21	so, that		

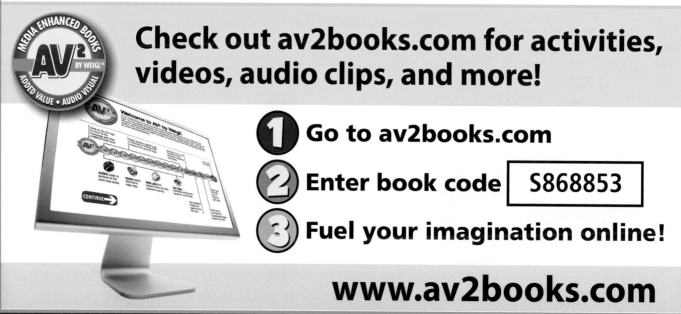